OTHER BOOKS BY

Ben Ditmars

Night Poems
Haiku in the Night
Inhale the Night
Sleeping with Earth
Number Poetry
Splinters
Moments at Midnight
Type 2

Susie Clevenger

Dirt Road Dreams
Insomnia's Ink
Where the Butterflies Pray
Splinters
Moments at Midnight

Susie Clevenger
Ben Ditmars

Cover Photos by Kim Stapf

All proceeds benefiting cancer research.

FRAGMENTS

Haiku and Verse of Seasons

Ben Ditmars

&

Susie Clevenger

For Tracy James Jones.

"And when the night falls
Before that day I will cry"

-Prince,
"The Most Beautiful Girl in the World"

Come, see the true

flowers of this pained world.

–Basho

Definition of *fragment*

: a part broken off, detached, or incomplete.

Definition of *season*

: the time when something specified flourishes, develops, takes place, or is popular, permitted, or at its best.

Introduction

What is a season? What's in a verse?
Authors Ben Ditmars and Susie Clevenger take you through the year with haiku and short verse poetry. Do you remember St. Patrick's Day, Halloween or Valentine's Day as a child or adult? Let these memories remind you of the love, pain and promise of each holiday.

Table of Contents

Valentine’s Day

Susie

hearts stalk February
with candy coated wishes
hoping dreams won't scar

Ben

there were paper cards
paper boxes and
my paper heart still bleeding

Susie

i painted my lips
february's bright crimson
love's feeding frenzy

Ben

did the red sea
of love and candy hearts
at long last part?

Susie

grocery store hearts
lackluster love expression
of forever's dream

Ben

oh, I miss a decorated
box with notes from
my admirers

Susie

Weighing Trust

the madness of intimacy
is pouring your soul
into another's heart
and trusting it will
keep your secrets

once the nightingale sings
it no longer controls the music

Ben

i cast off
expensive jewelry
candies
chocolates
for a chance at
lupercalia

rubbing blood
from milk-soaked wool
eager for the sacrificial knife
to cut deeper
than the lash

Susie

i'm the queen of hearts
royal cupid of choices
pain you encourage

Ben

before you buy me
chocolate boxes
or a chocolate rose
please know that
candy kills my heart

Susie

Icicle Flames

yearning is a cold fire
begging for heat,
a haunting valentine
frozen in ashes

gambling on romance
can bankrupt even the wise
heart chase addiction

Ben

no one buys me cards
on valentine's day
and maybe it is wrong
to hope for more
of them

St Patrick's Day

Susie

leprechaun chatter
of pinches for missing green
impish devilry

Ben

when warm winds blows
down leprechauns
i trade my thoughts of
snow drenched landscapes
for a green horizon.

Susie

hunt for bit of luck
clover leaves in counts of four
superstition's coin

Ben

living green means
more than just green beer
and shamrock shakes
it's real

Susie

a toast of green beer
for irish shenanigans
loosed with puckish glee

Ben

only you can
free me
from the snakes
when we
are green
against the world
without a golden
coin to spare

April/ Earth Day/Spring

Susie

Built on Nothing

the priest of self
gathered every
green and wild thing
to his ego and drank
their blood from
the golden cup of avarice

built on nothing the
temple shrine of glass eyes
crumbled into the heartless rape
of mother earth's soul
a lone seeker searches for light
and begs the sky to grant him mercy

Ben

oceans rise
storms surge and
the powerful
deserve to sink

Susie

Mother Earth

mother earth doesn't dream
of borders or bullets
to guard invisible
she spends her hours of insomnia
searching for a god humans haven't corrupted

Ben

to birds who suffer silently
inside nests of frost
breathe deep
repeat

Susie

Wren in Pearls

i'm dressed for clouds.
like a gray wren in pearls
i am a monochrome relief
pressed into sky arguing with sunlight

Ben

i'm undressed
and bare
to bathe in
moonlight and
a spring that never comes

Susie

tiny warblers dressed
in lemon chiffon feathers
summon rembrandts' brush

Ben

her soul is a flower
daring to be touched
before the sky grows dark

Susie

Artful Rain

rain falls in shades of monet.

cherry blossom brushstrokes transform
gray city sidewalks into watercolor interpretations
of spring

Ben

wind howls
like a luminous
landscape

a portrait
of van gogh

drenched in
oleanders

Susie

concrete monuments
wall the temple of visions
sky smothered in gray

Ben

lost in treetops
we are free as chlorophyll
inside of chloroplasts

Susie

thirsty pine trees moan
into drought's dust smothered wind
manmade disaster

Ben

a storm felled
the old oak tree
before we said
endlessly
goodbye

Susie

gasoline pipelines
artificial arteries
contracted by greed

Ben

i never saw
a pipeline growing up
but semi-trucks
were ventricles
and veins
to open as
we sang
the small town
blues

Susie

sunset turns my eyes
into watercolor sailors
searching the horizon
for the first blush
of summer's cheek

spring spreads origami wings
hoping to hold me in its spell,
but my heart turns toward
warm sand beneath my feet and
sea glass crumbs leading
me into salty waves
of ocean heartbeats

Ben

spring was not
my first love

i am born of snow
white paint
brush strokes
forming clouds

occasionally
i will find the ocean
in my tears

when the levee
breaks
and god
is warm

Easter

Susie

incense fed prayers
climb veins of stained-glass windows
reaching for savior

Ben

sometimes we pass over
violet shrouds
of self-denial

Susie

easter finery
parades for annual view
rabbit hat hopefuls

Ben

if only eostre
could see the
eggs we've
painted red to
celebrate new life

Susie

hidden pastel eggs
lottery search of small hands
part blades of green grass

Ben

eggs are symbols of empty tombs
rolling stones across your back
unstrapped

Susie

From Straw to Crown

i'm queen of my empty nest

shells of fledglings no longer haunt
nor memories sting when sunday's
sky is painted with wings' urgency

Ben

they never told us
painting easter Eggs
we were coloring
with borrowed time

Susie

Enter April

april, you place an umbrella in my hand,
a dance in my shoes, and watercolor tulips
to break the monochrome spell of winter

bless your days of sprouting green,
and raindrops urging me to blossom.

Ben

i see a chocolate rabbit
and I wonder if
it has a heart

Summer/4th of July

Susie

canines once served and protected
alongside their humans, but
the sounds of explosions
accompanied by laughter
is a much different hell

Ben

shots fired in the sky
were not kind to canines
wishing to protect

Susie

it will take more than a parade
our military sacrifice(d) so much,
yet while flags wave
in stars and stripes salutes
those who serve(d) try
to find peace with war
they can't forget

red, white, and blue flag
division in united
how long will it wave

wedding dresses bloom
in until death proclamations
season of i do

Ben

i hear names
called across oceans
echoing off mountains
refusing to be buried
in the sand…

"a father expecting three"
"a young man full of life"
"a hero from st. charles county"

Susie

Forever In July

we are july… long nights
of summer moon…
thirty-one days of forever.

let's not waste eternity by
dreading an august sunrise

Ben

we were sunburnt and alive
through hot girl summers
rising with the steam

Halloween

Susie

angel of mercy
flying a needle sky
clouded with corpses

Ben

i guess we dress up as adults
on halloween with unpaid bills
slung like marley's chains
around our necks

Susie

monsters ring doorbells
october’s sweet tooth pursuit
begs satisfaction

Ben

does my dog
understand all hallows eve
wearing skins
and lighting sacred bonfires
on samhain?

Susie

porch light announcement
candy pirates are welcome
mystic halloween

Ben

nature's first death
is orange
her hardest hue
to hold
on halloween

Susie

jack o' lanterns smile
as they watch geese flying south
ghouls rustle the leaves

Ben

we were lost inside a sleepy hollow
pumpkin patch
with heads intact

Susie

nightfall quilts my thoughts
with dreams of needle stitched moon
and mother's fury

Ben

we were pirates
pumpkins
superheroes
for a day
spent wishing
hopeful

Susie

a furtive black cat
walks across a picket fence
dark side of mirror

Ben

a lonely dog
wishes he were mysterious
in his reflection.

Susie

Dark Butterfly

i am the light in darkness,
wings grown in nightmare's loam.
in me is the dust of stars and the sun
breaking through the obsidian eye of monsters.

Ben

my body is less
a temple than a
rotted pumpkin
gutted dead

Thanksgiving

Susie

leaves lie abandoned
like forgotten jewelry
autumn sacrifice

Ben

i love every piece of you
like autumn leaves
defying the pale sky

Susie

spiced candle flames rise
conjuring winter spirits
to dance with shadows

Ben

as we share
a horn of plenty
and raise a glass
for capricorn
there is giving
there is thanks

Susie

dreaming of normal
is an empty glass or wine
void of thanksgiving

Ben

thanksgiving is for john
and nothing tastes the same
without him there

Susie

restless thanksgiving
memories haunt empty chairs
hands cling to prayers

Ben

it is thanksgiving
but the family
does not know
their last supper

Susie

days tried to destroy
yet I sit with november
and lift thanksgiving

Ben

my uncle is sleeping
between boards games
and the kids
have found
hors d'oeuvres

Susie

fall's umber paintbrush
erases green with broad strokes
faded leaves wither

Ben

haiku is lonely on thanksgiving
when no one
shares syllables

Susie

blessings feel empty
if only ink on paper
lists without heartbeats

Ben

i hear the oven
clicking
much like the
truck
that sat idle

Susie

move in thanksgiving
with open hands uplifting
expressing life's grace

Ben

we said grace each year
and now we don't
for reasons
i don't
understand

Susie

autumn's last hurrah
puddles of red and gold leaves
taunt the northern wind

Ben

if today were our
last autumn
would we open a
red vein in
yellow leaves?

Christmas

Susie

like migrating birds
the first snowfall of winter
builds frosty white nests

Ben

i see your migration
and raise you a fistful
of ice thrown
downwind.

Susie

red splashes of wings
decorate cedar tree limbs
choir of cardinals

Ben

carolers out in the snow
became our garlands in a
season of covid

Susie

torn wrapping paper
lies abandoned on the floor
last sigh of christmas

Ben

christmas tree lights
dim like our souls
after so many loved ones
fall like ornaments
onto the floor

Susie

tinseled trees shimmer
in the electric mood spin
of frantic whimsy

Ben

i remember
dying trees
inside that
needed some
shock therapy

Susie

christmas ghosts visit
rearranging emotions
tears waltz among smiles

Ben

before life caught up with me
i lived in vanity
melting like snow

Susie

come with open heart
embrace the season's magic
feel the child within

Ben

i miss warm sunlight
on a snowy day
warm enough to melt the chill
but cold enough to
keep the forts alive

Susie

the twinkle of hope
shines with innocent sparkle
waiting for santa

a yuletide listing
catalogues of naughty or nice
santa is watching

Ben

but is it santa
or jesus looking down
on a scarred
burned
earth?

Susie

a christmas prayer
that love will cover the earth
the heart speaks amen

Ben

i would trade each present
from my childhood to have one thing:
more time

Susie

christmas is noisy
giggles rattle the rafters
carols out of tune

Ben

we shook our
jingtinglers

we banged our
trumtookas

and it was
both too much

and not
enough

Susie

polyester flow
of twenty first century
faux candle noel

Ben

we gave knucklebones
and hunting knives
as gifts for
saturnalia

Susie

christmas snowflakes melt
into visions of santa claus
walking on water

Ben

swimming pools
are frozen picnics
wrapped in fleece
like we have tasted spring
again

New Year

Susie

champagne and endings
soliloquy of broken glass
severing old years

Ben

your heart
fell down
like us on new year's eve

if only times
were squared
and not divided

Susie

Leaving it Blank

a new year begs for resolutions,
a list of musts and never agains.
why plot failure in my best handwriting?
it's often the dream yet to come that writes its own path.

Ben

i scratched a list
of never agains
into my arm
and watched
the blood pool
into shapes
of things
to come.

Susie

red fades into black
thorned skeletons of roses
announce the new year

Ben

the clock struck twelve
we yelled
we drank
we almost
never kissed
each other.

Susie

So, It Begins

a new year
appears on my calendar
worn days refurbished

rising from wild seas
i look to hope
to bring me freedom

a few stars
write their exclamations
across the moon.

Ben

each new year's eve
we dance on broken shards
of glass feeling time cut deep

Susie

flippant january
pretends a calendar turn
is a magic wand

Ben

something always seemed
spiritual about turned
pages
in january

Susie

Month of Lists

january loves resolutions that morning
the eye with snow white lists, brags
she's the alpha tigress of new beginnings

Ben

an alpha tigress
has lists
whereas
a lone wolf
howls in isolation
at the seasons

Susie

Hoping for New Ink

the new year opens
its book of empty days
and waits for circumstances
to write their journal

Ben

i try to count
a year in numbers
gained…

36 million heartbeats

8.4 million breaths

1,333 kisses

and any one
of these alone is
far from trivial

Susie

Birthing January

glitter pours from
a clock announcing january's birth…
spirits pray to the sparkle eraser
worry doesn't time travel

Ben

we time travel
each year on december 31st
with nothing but a clock and
auld lang sang

ABOUT THE AUTHORS

Susie Clevenger is an internationally read author, poet, amateur photographer, and digital collage artist. She has authored four poetry collections including Dirt Road Dreams, and Where Butterflies Pray. Her work has appeared in the online Literary Journals, Yellow Chair Review, Visual Verse, and Poetry & Prose Magazine. Susie lives in Houston, Texas with her husband Charlie and two emotionally needy tabby cats.

Ben Ditmars is an author of surrealist short-poetry. He has written six poetry collections Poems, Haiku in the Night, et all.) and been featured in several anthologies such as Reflections and Mirrored Voices. He lives in Ohio with his wife and a dachshund who steals socks.

CONNECT WITH THE AUTHORS

Susie Clevenger

facebook: @susieclevengerpoetry

susieclevenger.com

instagram: @butterflysue70

twitter: @wingsobutterfly

Ben Ditmars

facebook: @benjaminditmars

benjaminditmars.com

instagram: @benditmars

twitter: @benditty

www.ingramcontent.com/pod-product-compliance
Lightning Source LLC
LaVergne TN
LVHW050332160826
845677LV00014B/3602

* 9 7 9 8 4 1 1 7 7 2 6 4 7 *